Stunts

Tony Norman

Copyright © ticktock Entertainment Ltd 2006
First published in Great Britain in 2006 by ticktock Media Ltd,
Unit 2, Orchard Business Centre, North Farm Road,
Tunbridge Wells, Kent TN2 3XF

ISBN 1 86007 849 4

Printed in China

Picture credits (t=top; b=bottom):
7T Royalty-Free/Corbis; 10B © A. T. Willett/Alamy;
15T © Royalty-Free/Corbis; 23T Buzz Pictures;
11T, 13T, 14B, 16B, 17T, 19T, 21T, 32 Red Bull

Every effort has been made to trace the copyright holders, and we
apologise in advance for any unintentional omissions. We would be
pleased to insert the appropriate acknowledgements in any subsequent
edition of this publication.

Content

Introduction

BMX bikers, inline skaters, skateboarders and snowboarders are all part of the world of extreme sports. They enjoy trying new stunts and practising until they get them right. These athletes learn to jump, flip, spin and twist through the air. They never stop looking for new ways to enjoy their sport.

FROM THE ROOTS UP

Extreme sports mean danger. If you do stunts on bikes, skates or boards, there is a high risk of getting hurt. Helmets and other items of safety gear are essential. Starter lessons from experts are a good idea. They teach the basic skills of the sport, so the beginner can learn the best techniques, right from the start.

ON THE UP

Interest in BMX biking, inline skating, skateboarding and snowboarding is growing fast. Millions of people take part, and most of them are young. They are willing to experiment to find new stunts. These extreme sports are always developing.

BMX riders test their skills on rough terrain.

BMX BIKES

INLINE SKATES

SKATEBOARDS

SNOWBOARDS

Skilled skateboarders can soar high into the air.

Many snowboarding tricks were first performed on a skateboard.

The X Games

The X Games – originally the Extreme Games – have been held in the USA every year since 1995. Extreme sports fans from all over the world come to show off their latest moves. They take part in many different events to win gold (first prize), silver (second prize) and bronze (third prize) medals.

X GAMES RECORD BREAKERS

Skateboarding: Tony Hawk (USA) completed the world's first successful two-and-a-half mid-air spin, also known as a 900, in 1999.

Snowboarding: Barrett Christy (USA) is the top Winter X Games athlete of all time. She has won 10 medals.

BMX: Dave Mirra (USA) has won 18 medals in the X Games Bike Stunt event. At the 2005 games he won gold riding a gold bike.

Inline Skating: Ayumi Kawasaki (Japan) became the youngest X Games medallist when she won bronze aged 12 in 1997. She went on to win three silvers and a gold.

Inline skating is no longer part of the X Games. It was dropped in 2005 because it wasn't as popular as other sports.

The X Games have helped to popularise stunts.

The Winter X Games have taken place every year since 1997.

SKATEBOARDING FACTS – DID YOU KNOW?

At the 2004 X Games, Danny Way (USA) set a new world record for the longest distance jumped on a skateboard. Danny jumped 24 metres (79 feet).

Left to right: inline skating, skateboarding, snowboarding, BMX.

TRUE STORIES
Los Angeles, 2003. Skateboarder Jake Brown (Australia) tried 20 times to do the '900' two and a half twist stunt at the X Games, but finally had to give up.

BMX

BMX means Bicycle Motocross. It started in California in the early 70s. A group of children copied their motocross heroes. In motocross, motorbikes race over tracks of mud or sand, jumping hills and twisting round tight bends. The first BMX racers did the same thing on bikes. The BMX craze soon spread around the world.

BIKE STYLES

There are three kinds of BMX bike:
Race: This bike is best for dirt track racing. The frame is light but tough. It has knobbly tyres to grip the dirt and a strong back brake.
Freestyle: This bike is great for BMX stunts and tricks. The front wheel can be twisted 360 degrees and the tyres are smoother. Ideal for the skatepark, or just riding to school.
Jump: Can be used for jumping ramps or riding country trails. Like a mixture of BMX and freestyle bikes. The tyres have the most tread of any BMX bike. The deeper the tread, the better the grip.

Dirt track racing needs a sturdy bike with good tyres.

Stalling a bike means to hold it still for a few seconds.

BMX FACTS - DID YOU KNOW?

Corndog sounds like something good to eat, but for BMX riders it means it means being covered in dust, often after a fall.

Racing bikes are lightweight, designed for speed over rough ground.

TRUE STORIES

London 2005. British BMX rider Ben Wallace worked with a scientist to create the Einstein Flip, a jump combining a backflip and tabletop, for a publicity stunt at the Science Museum.

Freestyle bikes have a sturdy frame, ideal for stunts and tricks in the park.

Combining strength with a light frame, jump bikes are great for dirt racing and jumps.

High Wheel Action

There are two styles of BMX tricks. Flatland stunts take place on the ground and often involve balancing the bike. Vert stunts need a ramp that is so steep it becomes vertical.

FLATLAND

Many stunts are done on flat ground.
Endo: The bike is balanced on the front tyre only.
Pogo: The rider stands on the back pegs, lifts the front wheel up and bounces up and down – like riding on a pogo stick!
Bunnyhop: The rider 'hops' by pulling the bike up so both tyres leave the ground.

VERT

Tricks that take place on very steep ramps are called vert stunts.
360: The rider and bike turn a full circle – 360 degrees – in the air.
Candy bar: The rider puts one leg through the arms and over the handlebars.
Tabletop: The rider leaps into the air, then pulls the bike sideways so it lies flat in the air.

Flatland tricks require a great sense of balance.

RACING FACTS - DID YOU KNOW?

The first skateparks were only for skateboards. Now some parks let bikes share the action. The ramps are also ideal for BMX vert stunts.

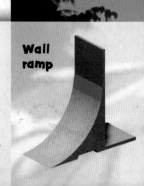

Wall ramp

TRUE STORIES

San Francisco, 2000. BMX star Dave Mirra made history by doing a double back flip in the X Games. He came first and won the gold medal.

A rider performs a can-can. He flips one leg over the bike so both legs are the same side, then goes back.

Fun box

Pyramid corner

Halfpipe

Dirt Jumping

Dirt jumping tracks are made of mounds of mud of different shapes and sizes. BMX riders ride up one mound, fly through the air, then try to land on another. The trick is to jump the first mound at top speed. This gives the rider enough height to do a mid-air stunt, before landing on the next mound.

DIRT JUMP STUNTS

Top dirt jumpers can do forward and back flips on their bikes, as they speed through the air. Another trick is the superman seatgrab. The rider comes off the bike in mid-air and holds on to the saddle. The body must be held out straight to look like Superman.

NO LIMITS

In X Games BMX dirt jumping contests, riders make a total of three runs round a set course. There is no time limit so riders can take all the time they need. The rider with the best tricks and jumps wins.

Trail riders encounter many jumps as they follow a set course through woods.

RACING FACTS - DID YOU KNOW?

The dips between the mounds of earth on a dirt jumping course are called canyons. Riders can be 4 metres (14 feet) above the canyon at the top of their jump.

The ABA (American Bicycle Association) rules state competitors must wear:

A superman seatgrab performed by Benny Korthaus from Germany.

TRUE STORIES

BMX dirt racing will be part of the Olympics for the very first time in Beijing, China in 2008.

enclosed shoes (not sandals)

a long sleeved shirt (or short sleeves with elbow pads)

long trousers (even if the rider is also wearing knee and shin pads)

a helmet. A faceguard is recommended but not required.

Inline Skate History

The first inline skates were made in the 1700s in Holland. They ran on wooden wheels. Today's skates have four or five plastic wheels, all in a straight line.

HOCKEY TRAINING

The first modern inline skates were made by brothers Scott and Brennan Olson from Minneapolis, US. They played ice hockey, but wanted to train in the summer too. They took the blades off their boots and added wheels and a brake. Later, they formed the company Rollerblade Inc., which has sold millions of pairs of skates all over the world.

INLINE STUNT SKATES

Stunt skates have four small, hard wheels that make them ideal for performing jumps and stunts. Plastic or metal 'grind plates' along the sides help to protect the wheels when the skates are used for stunts.

Vert ramps like this one are usually about 3 metres (10 feet) high.

This skater is balancing on the coping, the metal strip at the top of a ramp.

INLINE SKATER FACTS - DID YOU KNOW?

There are many kinds of races for inline skaters. Short sprints are skated by six competitors over 500 metres (546 yards). Distance races can be 25km (15 miles) long.

Recreational skates are comfortable and durable, ideal for the park.

TRUE STORIES

London 1760. Joseph Merlin made some inline skates with metal wheels. He wore them to a party and crashed into a big mirror. He did not know how to stop!

Racing skates have five wheels and are built for maximum speed.

Stunt skates give plenty of protection to the foot during tricks.

Buzz of the Blades

Like BMX riders, inline skaters are now welcome at many skateparks. They use the ramps to perform many stunts.

THE RAMPS

Inline skaters make good use of the halfpipe (a U-shaped ramp that looks like half a pipe), the vert (a ramp so steep it becomes vertical) and the coping (a metal strip at the top of the halfpipe wall).

THE STUNTS

Inverts: The skater travels up the wall, then holds on to the coping at the top and does a handstand, holding on to the coping. The body must be straight and still.

Front flip on vert: The skater travels up the vert backwards then does a front flip in mid air, before landing and skating back down facing front.

Railslide: The skater slides down a rail using the grind plate attached to the side of the skates.

Grind: The skater uses the grind plate on the skate to balance on a ledge, rail or coping. As the rider jumps down, the move is sometimes finished with a double spin.

Tomasz Piekarski from Poland practises a railslide.

A skater grabs the coping to make a turn.

helmet

INLINE SKATER FACTS – DID YOU KNOW?

Inline skaters keep their sense of humour, even when they get hurt. 'Road rash' is their joke name for the grazes and gashes they get when stunts go wrong.

TRUE STORIES

Brazil's Fabiola da Silva is a hero to every girl who wants to skate. Fabiola has won more X Games medals than any other female inline skater.

elbow pads

knee pads

gloves

wrist guards

Ride it Like a Wave

Skateboarding began in the USA in the 1950s. In the 1970s, a drought in California left many swimming pools empty. Local kids began to use skateboards on the slopes and walls of the pools. It felt like surfing on dry land.

Udi Hason does a handrail grind at the Street Dogs competition in Rome.

BEST BOARDS

The first boards were usually wider than boards today. Their clay wheels made them hard to control. Modern boards are made from a wood called maple, which is very flexible. Wheels are made from polyurethane plastic.

TOP MOVE

The ollie was invented by Alan Gelfand in the early 1980s. It looks easy but it's hard to do. Mastering the ollie is essential before other tricks can be learned. To do an ollie, the skateboarder stamps down on the back of the board and slides the other foot up the middle while jumping up in the air. It looks as if the board is glued to the skateboarder's feet.

Keeping control of the board is the mark of a great rider.

SKATEBOARD FACTS - DID YOU KNOW?

The world record for the highest ollie is held by Danny Wainwright of the UK. In 2000 he jumped 113 cm (44.5 inches) at the Ollie Challenge at Longbeach, California.

Many skateboarders like to make their own boards.

TRUE STORIES
Arizona 1998. Gary Hardwick from California took the world record for the fastest skateboard run. Gary hit a top speed of 101 kph (63 mph) during a race.

First choose the right deck.

Each board has two trucks that carry the wheels.

Wheels come in many sizes and colours. They fit on to the trucks.

Don't forget the correct bearings and the nuts and bolts.

No Time for Fear

Skateboarders need to jump very high in the air to do some stunts. There is no time for fear or holding back. The right equipment helps to give confidence. Helmets, knee pads, and elbow and wrist pads should always be worn.

Sandro Dias practises before a competition in Rio de Janeiro, Brazil.

WIPEOUT

A wipeout is a fall. Skateboarders are told to try to fall on the fleshy parts of the body, rather than on the head, hands or elbows. Relax and roll, that's the best way to deal with a wipeout.

MORE STUNTS

Kick flip Do an ollie, but flip the board around in mid-air before landing.
Grind Do an ollie to land on an edge or kerb. You will hear a grinding sound as you land and travel along. Do another ollie to come off the ledge.
Kick turn Push gently up a slope. As you reach the peak, lift the front wheels and turn through 180 degrees so you are facing in the opposite direction.
Rock and roll Rock the board on a ledge. End the stunt with a kick turn.

Skater's Point in California, USA, is a great place for skateboarders to try out new stunts.

SKATEBOARD FACTS - DID YOU KNOW?

Regular or goofy? Regular skaters stand with their left foot at the front of the board. Goofy skaters put their right foot forward. It just depends on what feels most comfortable.

Skateboarders can buy equipment to help them practise.

TRUE STORIES

Andy Macdonald from San Diego, California, is a world skateboard star. His advice for young riders is simple. "Don't do things to be 'cool'. Do what you want to do. Above all, have fun!"

A grind rail. This one is 1.8 metres (6 feet) long.

Portable ramp with textured surface to provide grip for wheels

Sticky-backed tape called griptape. It has a rough top side that helps riders to keep their feet on the board.

Skateboarding Fame

Tony Hawk, from California, is a skateboarding legend. By the age of 16 he was the best skateboarder in the world. He retired in 1999 after achieving the world's first two-and-a-half mid-air spin at the X Games. Tony now helps to promote the sport that he loves by building skateparks in poor areas.

GIRLS ON THE MOVE

More girls are enjoying skateboarding than ever before. One of the pioneers is Elissa Steamer from the USA. Elissa has been professional since 1998. She says: "When I started out I never saw other girls at the skatepark. Now girls see skateboarding on TV and they want to be part of the action. If they want to follow me, I'm happy. I love my sport."

SKATE AND SNOW

Snowboarding and skateboarding have a lot in common. Shaun White of California proves the point. In 2003 Shaun won gold snowboarding in the Winter X Games and came sixth skateboarding in the Summer X Games.

Elissa Steamer (right) and Evelien Bouilliart (left) won gold and silver in the 2005 X Games.

SKATEBOARD FACTS - DID YOU KNOW?

Skateboarding has its own words. Brain bucket – helmet. Biff – crash. Fakie – riding backwards. Carving – making turns on the skateboard. Bail – chicken out of a stunt.

The plan of a new skate park.

Sergei Ventura of Virginia.
USA is a professional
skateboarder known for
the hights he reaches on
a skateboard.

TRUE STORIES

1998. America's Billy
Copeland set the
world's fastest
skateboard run with
a speed of 112 kph
(70 mph). Billy got the
power from eight
petrol jets on the back
of his board.

Mounds of earth
form the ramps.

Concrete is sprayed
on to the base.

The surface is
smoothed out.

The finished skatepark
in Michigan, USA.

Snowboarding

Snowboards are light and range in length from 90–180 cm (3–6 feet), depending on the stunts they are used for. Freeride boards are for twisting and turning down mountain slopes. Freestyle boards are used for tricks and stunts. Freecarve boards are designed for racing at speed down snowy slopes.

Shaun White from San Diego, California, is as talented on a snowboard as he is on a skateboard.

HALFPIPE STUNTS

Some of the best action is seen in the halfpipe. This is the U-shape seen in skateparks, but it is made out of snow. Snowboarders slide down one side to pick up speed. When they hit the top of the opposite wall they jump and do stunts in mid-air.

McTwist: The rider performs a backflip with a twist in mid-air.

Straight Air: The rider does a half-twist in the air, then rides back down the halfpipe wall.

Grabs: The rider grabs the board during a trick. Some of these have strange names, like Slob Air, Stale Fish and Fresh Fish.

Goggles protect the eyes from the glare of the snow.

SNOWBOARD FACTS - DID YOU KNOW?

Snowboarding started in the USA in the 1960s. It has been an Olympic sport since 1998 and is now the fastest growing sport in the world.

There are three kinds of snowboard:

Slopestyle

Freeride boards are a great all-rounder, suitable for any mountain slope.

Freestyle boards are shorter, lighter and more flexible. They are best for twists and turns in the air.

Freecarve, or race boards are designed for speed on hard snow and are best for smooth turns.

Danger in the Snow

Snowboard parks are good places to learn new tricks. But freeriders want to test their skills in wild mountain areas. They speed down the slopes, flying over humps in the snow. When they come to a ledge, they jump out into mid-air and land on the snow below. These real-life stunts are a thrill, but there are dangers too. Riders need the skill to swerve away from trees, big rocks and steep cliffs.

AVALANCHES

Snowboarders fear avalanches. That is when a mass of snow falls down the mountain side. There is often no warning and the snow can travel at 120 mph. Snowboarders can start avalanches by riding in danger areas. New snowboarders are taught to recognise the conditions that are too dangerous to ride on.

Freestyle snowboarders push their bodies to the limit to get their stunts right.

SNOWBOARD FACTS - DID YOU KNOW?

In Canada and Alaska, expert snowboarders travel to the top of mountains by helicopter. They are dropped off at the top, and the only way is down – by snowboard.

The right equipment will be flexible and keep you safe.

SAFETY FIRST

Snowboard safety gear includes
a helmet, wrist guards, knee and
hip pads, goggles, gloves,
snowboard boots – and a mobile
phone. If a snowboarder is
caught in an avalanche, they
can use the phone to
call for help.

*Freeride snowboarders enjoy
the different challenges of
riding down a mountain.*

TRUE STORIES

Sister and brother Natalie and Chris Nelson
from California are two of America's best
snowboarders. They spend 200 days a year
working on new stunts on the snowy slopes.

Bottom pad
thin enough
to go inside
trousers.

Knee
protectors
and shin
guards.

Gloves
with
good
grips.

Hard helmet
with
detachable
ear warmers.

Around the World

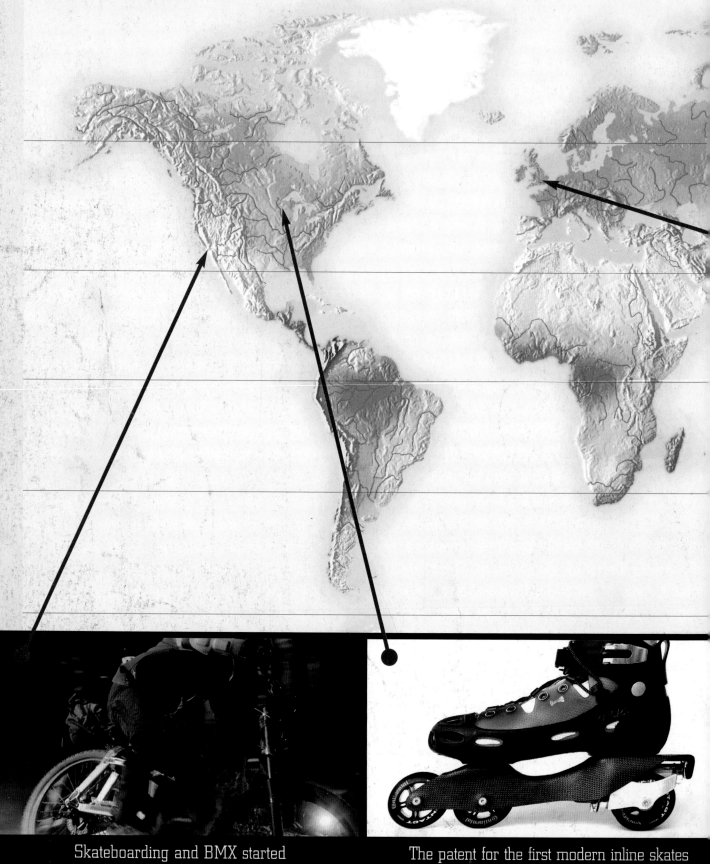

Skateboarding and BMX started in California.

The patent for the first modern inline skates were filed by Scott and Brennan Olson in 1979.

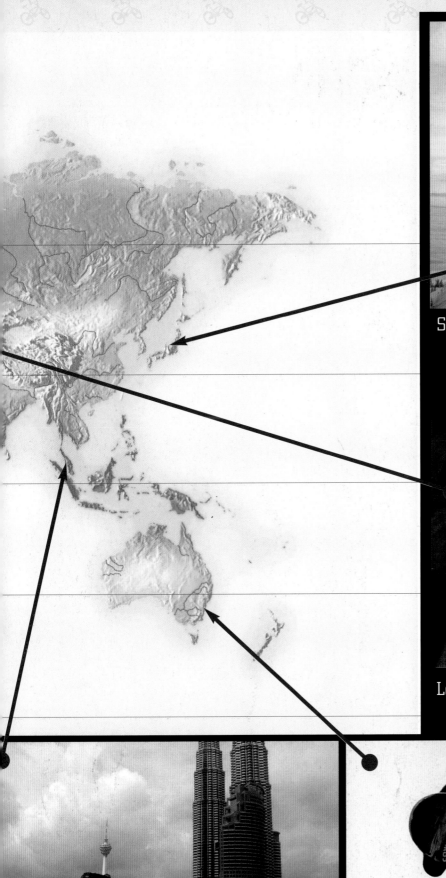

Snowboarding first became an Olympic sport in Nagano, Japan, in 1998.

London, UK, 1760. Joseph Merlin is the first skater on metal wheels.

Asian X Games have taken place in Kuala Lumpur City, Malaysia.

Skateboard star Jake Brown comes from Sydney, Australia.

Glossary

Athlete
A person who takes part in any kind of sport.

Bearings
Metal fittings that go inside the wheels of a skateboard to make them run more easily.

Blades
The sharp part of ice skating boots. Rollerblades are like ice skating boots with wheels instead of blades.

BMX
Bicycle Motocross, a type of sports bike.

Bronze
The colour of the medal awarded to a person or a team who wins third prize in a competition.

Coping
A metal trim at the top of a wall in a skatepark.

Deck
The curved wooden part of a skateboard.

Drought
A time when water is short, usually when there has not been enough rain.

Extreme
Something that is pushed as far as it can go.

Flatland
Name given by stunt fans to flat ground.

Flip
Turn over.

Full pipe
A piece of equipment in a skatepark that is shaped like a huge pipe. To do a full pipe, a skater has to skate upside-down.

Fun box
A four-sided jump with a ramp on each side, used for stunts.

Gold
The colour of a medal awarded to the person or team who win the first prize in a competition.

Griptape
Sticky-backed tape with a rough surface that is used to cover a skateboard, and helps the rider's feet to grip the board.

Halfpipe
A ramp that is shaped like a pipe cut in half lengthways.

Hardware
The nuts and bolts used to join together the parts of a skateboard.

Handrail grind
A skateboard stunt in which the rider slides the board along a rail.

Maple
A type of wood that is used for most skateboards because it is flexible and very strong.

Mound
A pile of earth used in BMX stunts.

Ollie
A skateboard stunt invented by Alan Gelfland in Florida, US in the early 1980s. Alan's nickname was Ollie.

Polyurethane
Tough plastic used to make skateboard wheels.

Quarter pipe
A small ramp that slopes gently.

Rollerblades
Another name for inline skates.

Silver
The colour of the medal awarded to the person or team who wins second prize in a competition.

Skatepark
A park with ramps where people can go to perform tricks and stunts.

Snowboard
A board like a skateboard without wheels that is used on snow.

360 degrees
A full circle.

Truck
A metal axle that holds the wheels under a skateboard.

Vert
Used to describe stunts done against vertical ramps.

Index